As a self-motivated, decidedly ambitious individual, Amna Al Hammadi has a strong understanding of equally local and regional customer and market dynamics. She brings over 18 years of experience working in the fields of diplomacy, strategy and communications in different industries, which gives her unique background and expertise.

In addition, Amna has strong communication, negotiation, interpersonal, leadership and consensus-building skills. She is Harvard alumna, specialized in leadership and management and holds an executive master's degree in international strategy and diplomacy from the London School of Economics and Political Science. Amna also holds a master's degree in marketing from Strathclyde University, UK; a bachelor's degree in applied media studies from the Higher Colleges of Technology; and an executive diploma in management from the Chartered Management Institute, UK. On the other hand, Amna is an ICF-certified coach.

Amna Al Hammadi

NATION BRAND: SOFT POWER AND THE CASE OF THE UNITED ARAB EMIRATES

AUSTIN MACAULEY PUBLISHERS™

LONDON • CAMBRIDGE • NEW YORK • SHARJAH

ISBN – 9789948766704 – (Paperback)
ISBN – 9789948766698 – (E-Book)

Application Number: MC-10-01-9014065
Age Classification: E

Printer Name: iPrint Global Ltd
Printer Address: Witchford, England

First Published 2024
AUSTIN MACAULEY PUBLISHERS FZE
Sharjah Publishing City
P.O Box [519201]
Sharjah, UAE
www.austinmacauley.ae
+971 655 95 202

I could not have undertaken this journey without my husband, Ahmad Al Khalidi, who was behind starting this book and starting my diplomatic career. Thank you.

Special thanks to the creative designer Norah Mohamed Al Thabahi for designing the book cover.

Table of Contents

I. How Effective Is Soft Power in Today's World?

It is fair to argue that soft power plays a seriously significant role in enhancing the reputation and apparent image of states, regionally and globally, and therefore also plays a major role in consolidating respect and love among the world's peoples.

Soft power is not only increasingly important to build a nation's image, both socially and politically, but is also the least expensive and most convenient and effective option in the long term to achieve the interests of a nation and enhance its position.

For years, countries have been leveraging this so-called soft power to preserve their interests and ensure their significant presence in various societies, and in the process, building a strong and positive nation brand that has a respected position in the international arena.

However, some leading states, for example, those involved in major conflicts, may have to set large budgets to invest in their soft power strategies, including cultural, academic and diplomatic projects, or propaganda activities such as far-reaching campaigns on social media, as part of a policy of controlling perceptions of the struggle with current or potential future opponents.

This type of strategy has already resulted in an accumulation of international, cultural and media relations and public opinion-making channels, and there are many partners to be found for those in decision-making positions who help to bolster certain economic and political interests and, when needed, act to relieve pressure.

Today then, soft power has become an essential method of influencing minds, winning emotions and getting to grips with people's behaviour, social trends and emotional tendencies.

Tolerance and acceptance of others with an open mind have been among the most prominent weapons in the rise of soft power, and with various methods, styles and forms of presentation, these facets have contributed greater success to the acceptance and promotion of soft power than the more traditional pattern used for decades, that of using force to make gains.

Once thought of as idealistic, the notion of soft power has gained far more traction in recent decades through broader scientific research and studies and has become increasingly popular due to the incredibly rapid and impactful socio-economic changes taking place around the world.

The influence of soft power does not stop at this point, but goes beyond it to deal with situations like international crises and challenges to official diplomacy which in the past may have supported force in some sensitive issues. In this way, soft power has provided alternative methods to reach satisfactory conclusions on economic agreements and treaties.

The establishment of alliances at the state level and the expansion of soft power is now a fundamental tool for many nations to increase their influence and significant presence on the international stage while enabling them to spread and secure their foreign policy and pave the way to attracting more allies.

In today's constantly changing world, building a nation's image or brand is more complicated, complex and sensitive than ever before. The image that an individual, institution, or even state creates for itself has become one of the most critical components in contributing to their success and the achievement of goals; building a society that believes in, respects and trusts a strategy of soft power is more important now than ever before – but this must be conducted in a way that *deserves* society's support, not demands it.

II. How a Nation's Brand Image Is Linked to Its Soft Power

In order to understand the connection between nation-branding and soft power, we need to analyse and then resolve the connection between strategy and implementation in building a strong and positive nation brand. In this way, we can demonstrate the importance and positive impact of soft power in building a nation's image.

Using the UAE as an example, the primary research question has to be: "How has the UAE's soft power been a major contributor to developing the solid international image that reflects the UAE's nation brand, and how do these competencies actually relate to the state's perceived position on the global stage?"

The UAE is building a solid and dependable reputation and understands that the most important means of achieving this goal is to analyse the priorities and preferences of the 'other parties' in order to achieve parity between their wishes and desires and those of the UAE.

a. Concepts and Theories

Power and the desire to rule are infinite concepts, since individuals, by their own human nature, will take on the responsibility of rule when handed that power. [1]

The philosophical "Leviathan" concept (Thomas Hobbes)[2] expounds that individuals, in their natural condition, are self-centred and anxious.

Researchers in international relations agree that having power means having the ability to control and influence others' behaviour in a way that serves their interests or to achieve the goals they seek.

Power has also been defined as "governing the man by the thoughts and actions of others"[3]. Realists trust that the desire for power is deeply embedded in human nature[4], fulfilling the need for government by social contract.

The modern realist school believes that power is a complex concept with a duality that combines goals and means. It is a goal when its purpose is to build the foundations that influence others' behaviour to improve their interests, and it is a means that helps the state achieve the ability to influence. Therefore, if the state wants to achieve a specific

---

[1] Francis Fukuyama. *The end of history and the Last Man*. London: Penguin Books, 2012. Page 245.

[2] Geoffrey M. Vaughan. "THE AUDIENCE OF "LEVIATHAN" AND THE AUDIENCE OF HOBBES'S POLITICAL PHILOSOPHY." *History of Political Thought* 22, no. 3, 2001. Pages 448–71.

[3] Morgenthau et all. "Politics among nations: The struggle for power and peace." 1985.

[4] Kenneth N. Waltz, *Realism and International Politics*. New York: Routledge, Taylor & Francis Group, 2008. Page 78–80

goal or goals, this concept is assumed to have the ability to achieve those goals, in the sense that it has the ability to combine material and immaterial factors. Furthermore, if the employment of potential factors could achieve the goals, the state would have achieved its interests[5].

Power is relative by nature because a state's power is measured by comparing it to other states. Power is also gradually emerging, which means that some relatively weak countries are able to play a significant role in a particular crisis quickly and unexpectedly, influencing another country more substantially than it may have otherwise and even force it to change its policy. That directs us to understand that human desire leads and controls power, actions and behaviours. The same applies to nations that are governed by individual desires that direct the nation's behaviour as a whole. Power is an individual's control over other individuals' ideas and actions.

Power is a natural political characteristic, but it is the product of material resources.[6] Power has a relative meaning, as the criteria adopted in measuring it are not the same as the standards adopted in measuring another country's strength. For example, the geographical position, the size and the nature of its resources; the efficiency of its political system and the quality of political leadership; the scientific and technological capabilities; and other factors adopted in

---

[5] Robert D Cantor. *Contemporary international politics*. West Group, 1986.

[6] Morgenthau, Hans Joachim, Kenneth W. Thompson, and W. David Clinton. "Politics among nations: The struggle for power and peace." 1985.

measuring the strength of any country, are difficult to evaluate accurately compared to these same aspects in another country.

On the other hand, force by its nature, is variable, not fixed and a change in the weight of its constituent elements leads to a change in the size and effectiveness of this force, as the state's power in its outcome is equal to the sum of the components of the force. It also varies within a country from time to time. With all its quantitative and qualitative components, power does not disclose its content and does not reveal itself except through the actions associated with it and the influence it brings to bear.

The quantity and quality of the capabilities available to the state are the means to measure the size and weight of the influence imposed on others to follow specific behavioural patterns on the superficial level. This includes the skill in mobilizing the goals of those capabilities and how to employ them to serve the state. The credibility, as well as the degree of need or dependence or the power of the state, does not depend on any specific element but on a permanent interaction between elements that do not necessarily have the status of stability.

The strong state can influence others' behaviour and attitudes in a way that serves its interests and achieves its objectives. The state's behaviour results from the interaction between several factors (material and moral), which may not be available or applied to the same standards in another state.

At the national level, states exploit their abilities and capabilities to achieve the goals they seek to achieve, increase their prestige and improve their relative position in terms of power and influence in the international system. Small states with limited capabilities might also have power elements in international politics that some of them can exploit. Their power may lie in raw materials or strategic locations, even though the importance of such elements and components is inferior to the level of capabilities and power factors in a significantly powerful state.

Despite the fact that many schools of thought and theories are concerned with defining power in international relations, power relates to one party's ability to influence another party to compel it to implement its will because it possesses fixed and variable elements that allow it to reach this desired result, knowing that the best means of obtaining compliance from others are the least costly and most influential.

States seek to harness power to protect themselves, expand regionally, influence others, or impose their policies. The objectives of each state in seeking to possess power vary according to its capabilities and geographical location.

Power in political science is the ability to influence others to achieve the desired results or compel others to act to serve the holder of power and influence the balance of his interests. Whether it is a party, group, or tribe, each state or actor can influence others' behaviour, and this can be done in three main ways:

1. The practice of threat and coercion, which we can call the "stick."
2. The exercise of temptations and bids, which we can call "the carrot."
3. Attract others to you, make their will conform to yours, and make their endeavours compatible with your goals, which we can call "referent power."

Decision-makers and opinion leaders will often target influential actors such as state institutions, the private sector, non-governmental organizations, society in general, sectors within society, or even individuals, and for this purpose, they harness all possible influences, including meetings, official visits, sports, arts, commerce, media, humanitarian aid, academic conferences, tourism, culture, and other factors that enhance the role of the state, its effectiveness and its presence in the international or regional arena.

b. Concept of Attractiveness

Based on the above general understanding of power, we can start defining what is meant by soft power, which began to gain currency around the end of the eighties of the twentieth century. The name was influenced by global technological development, especially in the rapidly expanding field of computer technology; however, almost all research shows that it owes its spread to the American writer, Joseph Nye, who held important positions in the US administration and is considered the inventor of "soft power."

Nye defined soft power as: "the ability to get what you want through gravity rather than forcing or paying money. It arises from the attractiveness of a country's culture, its political ideals and its policies." When our policies appear legitimate in the eyes of others, our soft power expands.[7] Soft power directs available choices based on the attractiveness of its social and cultural system and its value system. [8]

---

[7] Joseph S Nye. *Soft Power: The Means to Success in World Politics*. Public affairs. 2004.1–32.

[8] Nye. *Soft power: The means to success in world politics*. 1–32.

Soft power is more than just persuasion or the ability to win over people with an argument, although that is part of it. It is also the ability to attract, and attraction often leads to persuasion. This understanding of soft power was based on most of the opinions that dealt with the subject, which acknowledge that soft power is the ability to influence outcomes, and wanting to change the behaviour of others when necessary. It is the capability to obtain desired goals and change others' behaviour when necessary, wielding power in a soft capacity through persuasion and attraction and not coercion.[9]

Soft power is a state's ability to use means other than military to achieve its goals and interests, and among the most important of these tools and means are the media, cultural attractiveness and political values, to reach the stage of implementing these goals through the influence of enticement and seduction. Soft power is the power of attraction and polarization – it leads to getting others to respect your values and ideals and effectively do what you want them to, the ability to obtain the desired results through gravitational attractiveness by making others want what you want, using those intangible resources of cultural attractiveness and political values.[10]

In this context, some argue that soft power has a character, a positive standardizing ideal for the international and regional systems, and promoting opportunities to create a "damn society power." This force represents an essential

---

[9] Nye. *Soft power: The means to success in world politics.* 1–32.

[10] Joseph S. Nye Jr, *Soft power: The means to success in world politics.* 1–32.

brake on the international community and cooperative regional societies' "Power Curse," the theory that an overreliance on power can diminish the influence of nations. Considering soft power and how others view the possessor helps to weaken and alienate itself. On achieving the desired outcomes, threatening once fundamental interests and mobilizing other actors against someone, endangers the system's stability and continuity.[11]

As the concept of soft power picked up traction and spread, attempts were made to implement it by states other than the USA, such as Russia, China, Japan, Korea, India and the European Union, broadening the scope of its employment.

Among the most striking indications of the importance of soft power is that terrorist organizations, extremist movements, or non-governmental organizations have managed to expand across countries' sovereign borders mainly through their soft power.

Terrorism critically depends on soft power. Access to technology increases access to destructive power but also significantly increases communication capabilities across regions of control and to potential listeners around the world. Soft power depends on an audience willing to receive even if the transmitter is evil.

Trans-national terrorist organizations, such as Al Qaeda, maybe alienating most of the world, but it is attractive to some extremists. As for non-governmental organizations, they also have a soft power that helps them expand, as they are a global

---

[11] David W Kearn Jr, *"The power curse: influence & illusion in world politics by Giulio M. Gallarotti"* (2010): Journal of Power – August 2010, 275–282.

conscience representing a broad public interest that goes beyond the scope of individual states. No matter whether are allies or adversaries, these organizations are flexible and effective in penetrating countries without taking into account geographical borders.

The core of soft power is the ability of a particular nation to influence other nations and direct its available choices based on attractiveness, value system and institutions instead of reliance on coercion or threats.

c. Resources

Each type of power has resources that it uses to achieve its goal of obtaining submission to others. Despite the various writings that deal with this topic, Joseph Nye's writings remain the most prominent. Nye was the first to write about it in-depth and wanted it to be an anchor in building relations between countries, and he identified the sources of soft power as culture, political values and foreign policy.[12] Accordingly, a nation's soft power depends on these three primary resources. As for hard power, this depends on the use of actual force, whether in peace time or war.

So, soft power rests on the resources of culture, political values and foreign policies. The culture must be capable of being attractive to individuals and peoples of other countries when there is legitimate and moral authority. Popular culture that focuses on universal values and its policies promote values and interests shared by others; it increases the possibility of obtaining the desired results because of the

---

[12] Joseph S Nye. *Soft Power: The Means to Success in World Politics*. Public affairs. 2004.

relationships it creates from its attractiveness. Conversely, narrow values and limited cultures are less likely to produce soft power, and nations benefit from other global culture.

Soft power tools include political and cultural values, media capabilities, scientific and intellectual exchange, extending bridges, and establishing links and alliances. In contrast, hard power is based on coercion and force, and its tools are military capabilities and the ability to impose economic and political sanctions.

Political values form a critical source for soft power, and their impact depends on their compatibility in domestic and foreign policies and consistency, both at home and aboard. Hence, political values may not lead to direct political results unless they are adopted by the decision-maker as specific goals and thus become of great importance when the statesman effectively translates them, according to his perceptions of the environment, into a specific behavioural pattern. Main conditions can be identified for the influence of political values as a source of soft power: that international relations in which states should act as a global humanitarian character are credible and legitimate, both within the state and abroad.[13]

Nye's basic idea in his presentation of the concept was to assert the existence of another non-physical aspect of force. Its strength is the attractiveness derived from the country's culture, values and credibility generated by its consistent practices. These values, and the need to not ignore this aspect, focus on the physical and military dimensions and economics,

---

[13] Frederick Henry. Hard and Soft Power: The Paradox of "Winning the War of Ideas" in the 21st century, 29, 2005.

which have a central place in the literature on international relations and foreign policy.

Nye countered multiple academic critiques of the concept's lack of depth in academics, saying the simplification itself is not analytical, often referring to the need to read between the lines in order to reach such a depth.[14]

International sources of soft power include a willingness to contribute to multiple collective solutions: being part of global problem-solving and respecting international laws, norms, institutions and systems relies on equivalency in cooperation and hesitation in solely handling problems, respecting international agreements and commitments under, and a willingness to sacrifice national interests.[15]

In general, the different prevailing definitions of soft power can be accommodated between two contiguous ends. It ranges from the attractiveness of popular culture's manifestations in all forms of power other than actual military power. The narrowest definitions of soft power limit it to the resulting state power as the attractiveness of its media, films, music, novels, literature, sports and cuisine, its chains of restaurants, its costumes, its linguistic style and other works of art and elements of its culture.

This definition is not limited to the press or non-specialist circles, but it does manifest in academics, like the British historian Neil Ferguson, who knows soft power as the

---

14 Bially Mattern Janice. "Whysoft power" is not so soft: representational force and the sociolinguistic construction of attraction in world politics." Millennium 33, no. 3 (2005): 583–612.

[15] Giulio M.Gallarotti. "Soft power: what it is, why it is important, and the conditions for its effective use." *Journal of Political Power* 4, no. 1 (2011): 25–47.

influence on world politics through "unconventional forces such as cultural goods, considering that the effects of the spread of these commodities are Contradictory Commercialization," which Ferguson evaluates as a negative, generating feelings of admiration, attraction or jealousy, rejection and resistance.[16]

Based on the above theoretical analysis, it appears that there is a state of chaos in defining the meaning of soft power precisely. With the agreement that it means the power of attraction, persuasion and voluntary acceptance of submission to the opponent resulting from the strength of his model, confusion appears in determining its sources once the economic capacity is identified as one of the sources of hard power, as Nye defined.

In an attempt to address the issues of lack of focus on soft power resources as a whole, it does not reveal on its own how it influences others' preferences and behaviour. The analysis of soft power resources forces an emphasis on the sources of gravity and how it works, which is outlined as a property related to the subject's relationship with others which generates trust – understanding others' feelings and interests to stimulate their cooperative tendencies.[17]

One of the most prominent forms of soft power that states currently use to influence societies is holding conferences, whether between leaders to discuss their common issues or between educated elites or society's various components. This demonstrates an ability to take into account the opinions

---

[16] Ferguson Niall. "Think Again: Power." *Foreign Policy* (2013).

[17] Alexander Vuving. "How soft power works." *Available at SSRN 1466220* (2009).

and interests of others, and participate with them in forums, gatherings, and dialogues in international, regional, multilateral and bilateral events to encourage peace and peaceful approaches to address conflicts and disagreements, economic and humanitarian assistance, diplomatic support and the activation of public or grassroots diplomacy.

III. The Importance of Soft Power

Soft power refers to achieving international goals through persuasion and cooperation instead of using armed force or economic sanctions, and other forms of coercion.[18] The ability to influence and attract the parties concerned to the path that serves the interests of the state and its entity by using material and moral resources, away from coercion and threats; the ability of covert containment and soft attraction so that others desire to do what the dominant power desires without the need for the use of hard power. Soft power comes with its ability to influence elites and the public alike.

Today's world is rapidly changing and developing, and those who want to advance in technology and economy need to be open to others, so the time will come when all countries and peoples become exposed to each other, and then the effect of soft power will increase in a way unprecedented in human history.

Weaker countries will find in the sources of their soft power that they are besieged day after day until they reach one of two outcomes: either the development of particular soft

---

[18] Frank Vibert. "Soft Power and international rule-making." 2008.

power sources that enable them to continue to compete and influence others, or defeat in a way that makes them unable to continue their stubbornness and arrogance, so they lose their will and the interest of others in them.

IV. The Nature of Soft Power

The concept of power has always been associated with coercive practices, forcing others to act in a certain way. The concept of soft power opens the door to studying the ability to influence others' behaviour through attraction and containment and not through coercion.

We may understand soft power as the opposite of hard power in its military and economic dimensions, and we may understand it as the third side of the power triangle: coercive power, reward power and the power of inspirational objectives, equating to military power, economic power, culture power and ethics. The military and economic powers produce the power to both prevent and grant.

Soft power, while necessary, is an elusive concept. The number of people who look to the state for a role model can measure soft power. Historically, didn't millions look to the Soviet Union, Communist China and even Nazi Germany for inspiration? Where are the aspects of moral transcendence in these extinct models? Soft power is also the power of ideology, which may be useful or evil. Soft power is not always moral.

Military and economic capabilities are types of material strength measured in the number of military units, billions in output and economic surplus. The problem with soft power is the difficulty in measuring it straightforwardly. We feel soft power is present, but we cannot measure it.

According to the amount they hold, there are many attempts to measure soft power and arrange the world's countries. Because of the difficulties in measurement, global measures of soft power do not reach a level of ranking all countries in the world in the terms of how much soft power they possess, but are limited simply to the classification of the most countries possessing soft power, which even in the most ambitious accounting does not exceed thirty countries.

There are six levels of spheres of influence and the types of actions and practices that states can take to achieve gains or defend those achieved gains by using soft power. They differ from one country to another according to their resources and capabilities, and these levels begin with aid programs, like how the European Union sends aid to African countries and the aid that is sent to Syria. Some countries have local governmental and non-governmental organizations that they employ in the framework of their foreign policies or even as a populist path away from state agencies, such as the Red Crescent and Red Cross and the IHH Foundation in Turkey. Each institution differs from the other in its role, whether relief plans from the program's design and geographical spread or others. The religious dimension is an essential factor in directing these capabilities.

The second and third levels depend on the fundamentals of the state and society and their institutions and experiences, from language to the educational and health systems, to the craft skills possessed by the labour force, trade volume and other fields.

The fourth and fifth levels are the two levels of partnership and projects within a practical operational framework, such as trade and tourism agreements. Also included here is the inter-state visa system, which is a severe level, and military manoeuvres, which are considered one of the highest projects expressing soft power without violence or war, along with joint defence agreements and the purchase of weapons. A review of these criteria shows that there is therefore no soft power without military power and a strong economy and that the first countries in possession of soft power are the same as the world's foremost military and economic powers, with a few exceptions for cases such as Denmark, South Korea and Finland.

The analogy that is close to the congruence between soft powers on the one hand and economic and military power on the other raises a degree of confusion, so you do not know whether soft power has a unique and independent existence or is it merely a product of wealth and military power.

Military power may not be essential in the formation of the soft power of a state, but the economic power of the state and its possession of an efficient and effective administrative apparatus and regulatory framework that produces wealth and achieves the welfare of society are necessary conditions in the formation of soft power.

The difficulties in defining and developing the concept are compounded by the predominance of the intangible nature of its dimensions in terms of the power's resources, the mechanisms for exercising it, or its objectives; the direction you take is essential to changing preferences, perceptions and feelings.

A large part of the difficulties surrounding the analysis of soft power and its effects is due to its associations, particularly its dimensions related to gravity. Studying international relations with regard to the roles played and emotional investment is a relatively neglected area.

Despite the significant role of emotions in world politics, they have not received sufficient attention, whether in their study or in developing appropriate methodological approaches to dealing with them, notwithstanding some of the contributions made by empirical studies on psychology and politics. We must recognize the importance of striving to develop multiple approaches to study the different dimensions of emotional impacts, especially with the significance of the processes of communication, information presentation, representation and assimilation.[19]

According to the adjective definitions in linguistic dictionaries, soft power induces comfort and reduces tension and feelings of stress or suffering, facilitates employment and implies gentleness and moderation. This analogous approach may complicate the concept's proper definition; to see a decrease in the intensity of the possibilities of overlap and contradiction between academic and metaphorical meanings.[20]

---

[19] Rose McDermott. *Political psychology in international relations.* University of Michigan Press, 2004.

[20] Michael Marks. *Metaphors in international relations theory.* Springer, 2011.

The effective use of this force helps to contain destructive intellectual tendencies, extremist movements and aggressive states due to the international will that genuinely desires the achievement of international peace and security. The opposite is true when they are misused or when they do not possess the resources.

It embodies not only the power of governments but also the power of their people, which hands state the responsibility of creating well-organized governments, management, decisions and society, and it also hands people the responsibility to strive relentlessly toward development in the fields of higher and popular culture.

The attractiveness of the model in soft power requires the state to attract and persuade with its domestic and foreign policies, which means that repulsive and hateful policies will not be welcomed for those who want to have high-impact soft power.

It is not a blind force; although it is intangible, obtaining it is consistent with an understanding of the nature of the changes that are taking place in the international environment and the ability to adapt to these variables and prepare to compete with its influential units in order to smartly achieve the desired results for the state.

It is noted that a general nature characterized previous theoretical arguments and research in analysing power resources. It linked them to unlawful or non-consensual behaviour or exercise of force. However, there appeared to be several other arguments in this regard which tried to give more specificity and detail in the sub-component of each of the soft power resources, whether moral or material, economic or military.

Soft power, then, is an important concept, but it is also elusive, and it is more likely that soft power does not truly exist in the absence of an adequate measure of economic success and an efficient political apparatus and regulatory framework that lead society.

V. Nation's Brand – What Is Nation Branding?

Researchers and theorists have defined nation branding differently, based on the motivation, determination, or consequences behind branding a nation.

By combining the definitions of nation branding, nation branding is reshaping national identities[21] in order to enrich the nation's competitiveness,[22] perhaps by holding various types of cultural, political, sports and trade events and activities[23] in order to modify, enhance, or even revive a nation's image.[24]

Theoretically, the employment of nation branding strategies shows that security or wealth anxieties do not only

---

[21] Wally Olins. *Corporate identity: Making business strategy visible through the design.* Harvard Business School Pr, 1990.

[22] Simon Anholt. "What is a competitive identity?" In *Competitive identity*, pp. 1–23. Palgrave Macmillan, London, 2007.

[23] Eugene D Jaffe, and Nebenzahl Israel D. *National Image ND Competitive Advantage: The Theory and Practice of the country-of-origin effect.* Copenhagen business school press, 2001.

[24] Hlynur Gudjonsson. "Nation branding." *Place branding* 1, no. 3 (2005): 283–298.

determine nations, whether realism or liberalism-focused: nations' branding strategies are also driven by the importance of image, which matters most for the people in power.[25] Smaller nations enter the global scene via nation branding.[26]

A nation's branding can also be defined as applying corporate marketing concepts and techniques to countries to enhance their reputation in international relations and to build relationships between different actors not restricted by borders.[27]

a. What Is a Nation's Brand or Image?

Nation branding is different from a nation's brand. Nation branding acts as a tool that enhances the nation's image but does not invent it, since a nation exists with or without branding efforts. A nation's brand can be positive and trustworthy, or weak and vague.[28] What determines and builds an image requires strategic planning and efforts, and here, soft power plays a critical role.

A nation's image is one of the most important pillars and significant gains that it considers when positioning the nation on the international scene. The image of organizations,

---

[25] Christopher Browning. "Nation Branding, National Self-Esteem, and the Constitution of Subjectivity in Late Modernity." Foreign Policy Analysis. 11. 10.1111/fpa.12028. 2013.

[26] Keith Dinnie. *Nation branding: Concepts, issues, practice.* Routledge, 2015.

[27] Pauline Kerr and Geoffrey Wiseman. "Diplomacy in a Globalizing World: Theories and Practices." 2013.

[28] Ying Fan. "Branding the nation: What is being branded." Journal of Vacation Marketing, Volume 12, No. 1, 2005.

nations in this case, dramatically impacts the targeted audience and can achieve many advantages in the long and short term.[29] Interest has increased in the image's topic and its importance for societies and organizations considering the value that it plays in forming opinions, establishing real impressions of them and creating positive behaviour in individuals toward the institution. Formulating the right image has become a goal that most organizations pursue to achieve their desired outcomes. Accordingly, studying and measuring this image is crucial to building policies and strategies to develop it.

A positive nation brand or image leads to economic and political benefits. Nations with a positive image and reputation attract investors, gain other nations' endorsement of their political actions, and build trustworthiness with other nations and individuals.[30] Additionally, optimistic nation brands establish brand loyalty with individuals by adding emotional and trust factors to their provided services, products and actions.[31] A nation's brand is used to endorse the state's economic and political interests, locally and internationally.[32]

A nation's image is relatively changeable, as its formulation is a dynamic process that changes according to a

---

[29] Lee Hastings, Bristol. *Developing the corporate image: A management guide to public relations.* New York: Scribner, 1960.

[30] Simon Anholt. "Nation As Brand." Journal of Brand Management 9 (4–5): 229–239. 2002.

[31] Wally Olins. "Branding the Nation – The Historical Context." Journal of Brand Management 9 (4–5): 241–248. 2002.

[32] Jim Rendon. "When Nations Need a Little Marketing," New York Times. 2003

variety of factors; social, political, economic, cultural and psychological, but this does not mean that it has lost its stability, especially if the messages the audience receives corresponds to the mental image it projected about the source of those messages. Many contradictory features and attributes can also characterize a nation's brand or image; for example, inaccuracy, resistance to change, generalization, ignoring individual differences and creating a biased perception.

Many researchers have argued that a nation's image is never accurate, and the reason for that is that it is mere impressions that are not necessarily formulated on an objective scientific basis but rather a simplification of reality. An image does not necessarily express the absolute reality of a state, but rather expresses it most of the time it is about a part of the overall reality, especially since people usually resort to forming an idea that are individual from others due to the scant information they obtain due to their inability to collect accurate data.

All activities carried out by a nation within the framework of international public relations are aimed at building, consolidating, or correcting the nation's image. Nations' brands vary from one country to another according to many considerations, including humanitarian, historical, geographical, or economic factors, which are the fundamental sources of soft power.

A nation's image is the set of judgments, perceptions and positive and/or negative impressions that it forms. This set creates the foundations of an individual's decision about this nation and determines his or her behaviour toward the nation. A nation's image can also be described as the map through which a person can understand, perceive and interpret things, the ideas that an individual creates about a particular topic, and the consequences of those actions, whether positive or negative, through which the behaviours of different individuals are formed about a nation.

b. Determinants of a Nation's Brand

We can see then that a nation's image reflects a series of political, social and economic issues that create a significant determinant and direct the nation's image either positively or negatively. In that case, a nation brand performs similarly to putting on cosmetics to cover an injury – it makes patients look in good shape, but does not cure the underlying cause. [33]

An image change or enhancement maybe required due to improper behaviour or events, or historically inaccurate or misleading information, creating a need to restore people's confidence. When a specific country wants to enhance its image in the international community, it seeks to build confidence in it as a peaceful country that is positive and cooperative in the international community and trustworthy in international events and interactions.

c. How Soft Power Constructs a Nation's Image

A nation's brand is structured on investment, tourism, political decisions and cultural aspects.[34] Similarly, Nye's soft

---

[33] M. Riston. "Liechtenstein's Five Steps to Superficial Change," Marketing Journal, 2004.

[34] Anholt S. "Nation-Brands of the Twenty-First Century," Journal of Brand Management: 395–406, 1998.

power concept states that a nation's soft power is structured on three fundamental sources: its foreign policies, culture and political values. Both nation-branding and soft power then are structured on common aspects.

Soft power as a concept might look modest to employ, but the employment and assessment of soft power are more challenging contrasted to hard power.[35] Soft power means the ability to persuade and make others do what you want, and not what they want by conviction, not by coercion, by agreement, not by intimidation, by attraction rather than by pushing, influencing public opinion and social opinion, and using soft power to change public opinion on an issue through channels such as civil society organizations.

Soft power and nation brands are relatively new concepts, and both are structured on the perception of individuals and how to go about changing this perception. Soft power is a nation's image backbone, as it sets the structure and builds the nation's brand image through its projects and initiatives. A nation's soft power can result in an optimistic nation's brand through its attractiveness and thus lead to political influence and the achievement of desired goals by enhancing its image.[36]

As the power of appeal, attractiveness is implanted in a nation's brand. The image and attractiveness rely significantly on the strength of a nation's domestic and

---

[35] Jonathan Mcclory. *A Global Ranking of Soft Power*. Portland: Portland's in-house Content & Brand team, 2018.

[36] Peter Van Ham. "Place branding: The state of the art." *The Annals of the American Academy of Political and Social Science* 616, no. 1 (2008): 126–149.

international values and policies, which are the sources of soft power. This image and attractiveness not only enhance the external strength of the state, but also bolster its internal strength by enhancing the confidence of its citizens in themselves, their political system and their future.

A nation's image can be defined as the total of an individual's thoughts, feelings and beliefs.[37] It is a process and an interaction that goes through multiple stages; each stage is affected by what precedes it, and by what is attached to it, as it is evolving and changing; and this takes many forms. This process is cognitive; it passes through stages of the cognitive processes of perception, understanding, remembering and subjecting to the variables and factors that such cognitive processes are subject to or are affected by. Moreover, this process is psychological; it has emotional aspects in addition to logical dimensions.

d. Empirical Background – Soft Power Through History

In what may seem a contradiction, the concept of soft power did not just suddenly appear in the world of international relations at the end of the 1980s. Despite many researchers' enthusiasm that the concept of soft power is new, research into the history of ancient civilizations confirms the tendency of several eastern empires to use it. Like the Pharaonic civilization, archaeological finds proved that Egypt's ancient rulers were promoting their rule in conquered

---

[37] Philip Kotler and Kevin Lane Keller. "Marketing Management. New Jersey: Pearson Prentice Hall." (2012).

areas by spreading sovereignty symbols, such as the golden beetles discovered in Palestine and Syria.

It is the name that is new, while the concept is indeed ancient and extends to the early beginnings of the emergence of empires and states, and we see examples among most rulers. The prominent people in Mesopotamia since the third millennium BC, Sargon of Akkadian and Hammurabi the Babylonian, used to extend their influence over different countries via their worship and cultures, they kept their gods and showed appreciation for them, as well as respecting their general culture. They approached them through intermarriage and seemingly benign laws.

In addition, the Persian civilization established monuments in captured areas of the Fertile Crescent. Archaeologists describe it as "political propaganda," the rulers indicating their compassionate greatness, and the same thing happened after the Romans invaded the eastern and southern Mediterranean regions, which is evident in Roman amphitheatres and other buildings.

The Islamic military campaigns in the seventh century AD are another example that emerges through the religions' historical progress. Through their expansion and spread, Islamic military campaigns formed the basis of an ideal soft power model that could penetrate the fortresses of the most powerful empires and the most closed cultures. The Islamic military campaigns did not rely solely on the power of the sword, although the use of the sword was often a cause for criticism as its use cannot be disputed, but these campaigns' lasting victory was in the strength of their values that created gravity and acceptance of the pre-eminence of the model that it represented, serving as an indication of the strength of the influence of this model that it ended forever the political existence of the Sasanian Empire in Persia (now Iran).

Our history bears witness in many eras that forces which have demonstrated the characteristics of combining a sufficient formidable force with an influential soft force are the forces that achieved a wider spread and a longer historical continuity, and even the effects of their soft power remained influential on the stage despite the decline of their formidable power.

The forces that relied purely on their substantial power in deploying coercion on others were fleeting. For example, the terrifying and destructive power of the Mongols that was able to sweep the world and subdue many peoples extremely quickly, but in the end, a whole empire ceased to exist and their stories are consigned to history books.

The Mongols' authority was undermined by the fact that they were primitive people who did not have the fortune of culture and civilization to bestow on others. The Mongol leaders at the time may have wanted to acquire the acquiescence of others through horror tactics, assuming that this would be a successful policy in achieving their desired results, but what they obtained from enforced obedience was not permanent, and was removed with the disappearance of the opponent's hard power. History has many similar tales to those of the Mongols. The propaganda launched by some of them, such as Al Qaeda, ISIS, other terrorist organizations, tyrants, despots and their ilk, may have had some effect of soft power that helped to gain followers and supporters, but within the framework of the role and the actual level of influencing soft power, it is limited and cannot be spread.

e. Soft Power and Nation Branding Examples

Nation-branding is a developing field in which researchers continue to search for a unified theoretical framework. Many countries aim to improve their country's standing as the image and reputation can significantly affect its economic viability, so nations seek to attract tourism and investment capital, increase exports, attract a talented and creative workforce, and enhance their cultural and political influence in the world. The various ways a country markets its trademark include exports, foreign direct investment, and the leisure industry.

A perfect example of product export is Germany, famous for its automotive industry because of prestigious car companies such as Mercedes, Audi, Porsche and BMW, while an example of foreign direct investment that helps a national brand is American companies that contribute to building overseas hotels, leisure centres or shopping malls and other European countries with manufacturing facilities in a number of different countries.

Countries are now moving toward the institutionalization of soft power, as experience has shown that real impact stems from creative government actions, practices and policies and the launching of creative humanitarian initiatives, not from slogans and promotional campaigns. Many countries are working hard to pay attention to this power, for example, the establishment of 200 British Council offices in 100 countries with the explicit aim of promoting Britain's role in international cultural and educational opportunities, and the German Goethe Institute now includes 159 global centres, reflecting the state's great interest in soft power, strengthening its reputation, and establishing its respect and affection among peoples.

Nations are beginning to have less interest in military force and economic sanctions that come with a financial cost. As an alternative, soft power resources and tools become the solution to achieve the desired results locally and internationally. Nations are moving toward developing those resources strategically to build dependable nation brands.

China invests billions of dollars in improving its soft power, but it still falls behind many western countries. China has 700 Confucius Institutes distributed throughout various countries, boosting its reputation in many African and Latin countries, but Europe and America's outlook is not optimistic due to the overall impression of autocracy in China, the lack of press freedom, the lack of public freedom and limited access to information.

Soft power has an effect on attracting tourists and reviving the travel sector for nations by promoting it through artistic or cultural channels. Some countries have succeeded in reaching large segments of foreign tourists through films or television dramas.

Turkey is one of the countries that have been able to promote their tourism sector through dubbed TV serials, with local reports indicating last year that the Turkish series ranked second in the world after the United States.

Turkish academics say that Turkish "soap operas" are exported to 102 countries worldwide, with Arab countries at the forefront of their import market. However, those interested in the Arab cultural arena do not hide their dissatisfaction with what is seen as a systematic intellectual invasion aimed at polishing Turkey's image.

An interest in form characterizes the majority of Turkish drama. From attractive filming locations and actors to issues that stimulate the viewers' emotions, such as romantic topics, these shows are dubbed into Arabic using a Syrian dialect, the same dialect in which the most successful Syrian dramas were presented, which has played a major part in Arab viewers accepting and fervently following the shows.

Turkish dramas do not neglect the promotion of tourist areas, which became popular after the broadcast of these series and became a destination of choice for Arab tourists.

Some people interested in art consider that any country's publishing or promotion of its cultural projects is legitimate. For example, regionally, the Kingdom of Saudi Arabia is actively rebuilding its nation's image through promoting its culture, values, tourism and attracting investment.

However, others believe that the media-led spread of Turkish series in the Arab world results from the deliberate allocation of considerable budgets to promote them and boost acceptance of a Turkish approach, led by the Justice and Development Party.

Whatever you believe, it is fair to say that the media plays a crucial role in promoting soft power.

VI. UAE History and Future Aspirations

Over the past seventy years, news of conflicts, wars, death, destruction and foreign interference dominated the media scene and news headlines in the Middle East, and the region was classified as a "political hotspot." This painful situation resulted in the migration of large numbers of distinguished Arab cadres to a better and more stimulating work environment, which deprived the region of its efforts and affected its development programs.

The United Arab Emirates, a young country with a population of nearly ten million people. The UAE has an influential and effective army, in training and active personnel. The UAE ranks 12th in the world in oil production and has excellent natural gas reserves.

With the emergence of the UAE's status and its successes in conquering the seemingly impossible, reaching goals that no one had previously attained in the region, the appearance of the Middle East changed, and other more positive news made the headlines. The UAE, in just a few short years, has turned into a success story and become a beacon for excellence, innovation and hope.

In the year 2020, during which the world found itself up against the challenge to control the Corona epidemic, prevent its spread and stimulate the economy, we find the UAE successfully launching the Hope Probe to reach Mars. It also succeeds in commencing operations of the Barakah nuclear power plant and introducing nuclear energy into the nation's energy mix.

The UAE now ranks among the countries exploring space, the countries that operate peaceful nuclear energy, and the pioneering countries in sustainable energy. The UAE has the ambition, planning and hard work to achieve all this, consecrating a successful Arab model and sending a hopeful message to the world. The UAE looks to the future, from its adoption of nuclear energy to its scientific ambition on Mars, by walking amongst the leading powers like the US, Russia, Japan and China.

a. UAE – A Soft Power Strategy

Like other nations, the UAE has shown apparent interest in soft power strategic planning and implementations to create attractiveness for the country and build a nation brand that attracts investment and tourism.

By the end of 2017, the UAE government had implemented the launch of its "UAE Soft Power Strategy," which constitutes a comprehensive national system that seeks to enhance the UAE's reputation and its brand image, regionally and internationally.

The strategy aims to cement the UAE's brand image as an economic, cultural, humanitarian and civilizational force, establishing its enthusiasm and admiration among all peoples worldwide by highlighting its image as a nation open to all cultures and civilizations. The UAE has the economic, cultural and sophisticated elements to build a global position and a reliable brand image. The UAE believes in the importance of soft power and has launched many initiatives in support of the concept.

The UAE Soft Power Strategy constitutes an integrated framework that embodies the UAE's status and respects its history, indicating that the comprehensive vision put forward will consolidate attractiveness. The strategy is based on a unique vision that the UAE is a significant gateway to the region, where cultures and ideas converge in an environment of respect, tolerance and human brotherhood. The strategy is based on the UAE's historical and cultural components, economic projects and humanitarian initiatives.

The UAE Soft Power Strategy aims to prepare a comprehensive governmental system in the Emirates to develop sustainable work programs and policies and implementation frameworks with both Arab and global dimensions, taking into account the country's economic, cultural, artistic, touristic, humanitarian and societal components, with an emphasis on the human and civilizational weight that the state enjoys. Building on the reputation that it has established for almost 50 years since its establishment as one of the most tolerant and open countries in the region and an intellectual meeting point between different peoples and cultures.

In terms of opportunities, soft power and building reliable and robust nation brands have helped UAE businesses achieve sustainability within the global market by considering appropriate policies and strategies. Going global improved the UAE education system, hospitality, entertainment sectors and generating a showcase for the Emirati culture. As a result of the continuous deployment of soft power, the UAE's international reputation and image continue to rise.

b. Tolerance as a Way of Life

The UAE is a country of tolerance and peace, and its laws have not only guaranteed justice, respect and equality for all, they have criminalized discrimination, undermining the causes of discord and disagreement. This dedication to openness qualifies it to become a global capital in which the East and West civilizations meet, promoting peace and rapprochement between all peoples.

The UAE is a pioneer in institutionalizing tolerance through the enactment of legislation and laws and the launch of local, regional and global strategies, initiatives and programs that make tolerance a tangible approach for all segments of society. The setting up of a National Committee to Combat Terrorism, laws to combat discrimination and hatred, and the establishment of the first Ministry of Tolerance, the International Institute for Tolerance and an international award for tolerance demonstrate the long-held belief of the UAE's wise leadership and government that tolerance is a way of life.

The UAE registered a new global framework in promoting interfaith dialogue through the historic visit of His Holiness Pope Francis, leader of the Catholic Church, to the country, when he presided over a historical mass in which tens of thousands of people participated at the Zayed Sports City Stadium. During His Holiness' visit, the Document on Human

Fraternity for World Peace and Living Together was issued, a joint statement signed by Pope Francis and Sheikh Ahmed el-Tayeb, Grand Imam of Al-Azhar in Abu Dhabi, the capital of global tolerance.

The UAE launched the first Ministry of Tolerance in the world, in addition to enacting legislation and laws that preserve freedom and respect for religions, in addition to the anti-discrimination and hatred laws.

The United Arab Emirates also recently announced plans to build a beacon of mutual understanding, harmonious coexistence and peace among people of faith and goodwill that brings together the three major monotheistic religions: Christianity, Judaism and Islam. Called the Abrahamic Family House, it will be constructed on Saadiyat Island, the cultural heart of Abu Dhabi. The Abrahamic Family House is not the first step the UAE has taken to promote tolerance values, as the cornerstone was laid for the first Hindu temple in Abu Dhabi in April 2019.

The UAE's education system also represents a model for tolerance in Emirati society, as it embraces employees of various nationalities from many different countries around the world, exchanging knowledge and cultures with students. Students are also encouraged to adopt volunteering as a graduation requirement, as volunteering represents the global face of tolerance.

The UAE is hosting Dubai Expo 2020 (moved to 2021 due to the Covid-19 pandemic), the largest global event of its kind, which confirms the success of the UAE's approach and policy in promoting humanity and the values of civilized communication between countries and individuals, in favour of building safe and cooperative societies that contribute to human development.

c. Human Aid Efforts – Risks and Propaganda

Since the emergence of the coronavirus (Covid-19), the UAE was quick to announce its support with the rest of the world facing the pandemic by providing a variety of support and assistance. UAE aid constituted 80% of the total global aid that reached the region's most in need, as the first defence lines benefited everywhere around the world. Active in vaccine research, manufacturing, storing and distribution, UAE aid continues to limit the spread of the new Coronavirus, which reflects its important humanitarian role and image at an international level.

There are, however, political risks whereby foreign aid proponents can have their image tainted due to various influencing factors, including negative propaganda. For example, where foreign assistance is accused of being strategically designed to serve the donor country's economic interests, such has been levelled against the UAE,[38] when a state gives official development assistance to a recipient country but the financial assistance is used to purchase luxury goods and services from donor countries. The development assistance has the conditions that a beneficiary state must purchase some overpriced donor goods. Another factor is where foreign aid is designed only to benefit specific

---

[38] A. Shah. 2014. http://www.globalissues.org/article/35/foreign-aid-development-assistance.

influential domestic interest groups.[39] These issues influence the impact that foreign aid will have on the security of a beneficiary state. Hence, countries such as Yemen, for example, receive financial aid from the UAE, but the country's security status quo remains the same. The rising cases of terrorism have propelled the UAE to increase its contributions through foreign and humanitarian aid[40] and the benefit of this aid, in this instance, was undermined politically to affect the UAE's image negatively on the global scene.

These attempts have not deterred the UAE from continuing to contribute to the efforts to combat the Corona pandemic and extend a helping hand to countries worldwide to help contain the epidemic. In addition to supporting the scientific efforts to produce medicines and vaccines to help eradicate this epidemic, the UAE spreads goodwill, extends a helping hand wherever it is needed, knocks on doors that have not been opened before, and offers various solutions to address the challenges facing the Arab world, and this stems from the UAE's commitment to the future of this region.

d. Political Initiatives from the UAE

The Palestinian-Israeli conflict has been a central issue in the Middle East region for many years and one of the reasons behind the tension and disagreement in it.

---

[39] M. Kanna. 2014. "Emirati foreign aid: Overview and foreign policy implications" Undergraduate honors thesis paper 35. https://scholarworks.wm.edu/honorthesis/35.
[40] UAE Government, Portal. 2019. "The UAE Soft Power Strategy." The United Arab Emirates' Government portal.

The conflict that began with the end of the Second World War and the declaration of the State of Israel on Palestinian territories was the beginning of a new historical stage for the region that transformed the conflict from Palestinian-Israeli to Arab-Israeli. The Arab countries supported the Palestinian cause in various forms, and the Gulf States carried the bulk of this support.

The Israeli side continued to annex more Palestinian Authority lands, restrict the lives of Palestinian citizens, prevent them from praying at the Al-Aqsa Mosque, and threatened to annex even more land.

Emirati diplomacy came to the forefront of efforts to break this deadlock in the Palestinian-Israeli situation and announced the establishment of full normal relations between the UAE and Israel with provisions to halt further annexation of Palestinian Authority territories, the opening of the Al-Aqsa Mosque to Palestinians and Arabs, and the rapid initiation of areas of cooperation in various sectors, contributing to the prosperity and economic growth throughout the Middle East.

The announcement of the establishment of relations between the UAE and Israel thus marks the beginning of a new phase of Arab-Israeli relations based on cooperation, harmony, and the strengthening of efforts targeting the Middle East's welfare and prosperity, not only between governments but also but between the peoples of the two countries.

This declaration represents a real opportunity for coexistence and cooperation to achieve prosperity for the region. It contributes to creating a culture of peace, tolerance and acceptance. It also contributes to strengthening the region's aspirations to be a source of achievement through innovation, building the future, and uniting efforts to meet the challenges that have hindered growth and prosperity in the region.

Life is full of opportunities, and the UAE, with its successful diplomacy, inspiring leadership and the determination of its people, can seize these opportunities. It is no surprise, therefore, that this agreement between the UAE and Israel is being attacked by entities and people who do not want growth and stability in the region, an exit from the state of "non-peace and non-war," which has dominated strategies and prevented growth over the past decades. The time has come to change how we all deal with the Israeli situation and start looking at Israel as a partner in the region's growth and prosperity and not as its enemy. These disputes often occur between countries, but every dispute has a solution in general international law provisions.

Looking toward the future and planning for it needs people to make courageous decisions and adopt bold solutions to change the stalemate in the Middle East so that together we can face the challenges that the region faces in different sectors. We can start by looking at the unification and integration of efforts as a means to advance the process of growth and prosperity in the region through a series of agreements and work programs.

Establishing normal relations with Israel represents a success for all parties involved in concerted efforts and employing them to best serve the region. The Arab countries and Israel live in a region that shares several similar characteristics, and working together will bring immense benefits to everyone. Many Arab states tried boycotting Israel and Israeli products for many years, but the boycott did not guarantee the Palestinian people's rights. Therefore, some Arab countries took the brave initiative to establish diplomatic relations with Israel.

Establishing relations and creating cooperation in various fields is already opening more doors, revealing more mutual interests, and exposing more channels for resolving issues that are still pending between Palestine and Israel, and this is what the United Arab Emirates seeks. The peace agreement between the UAE and Israel was widely declared as an essential step toward establishing rules for peace in the Middle East region.

e. The UAE and Soft Power

The UAE is portrayed as a dynamic Arab country that wants to do away with many obstacles, partly because a complete view of the world from a purely Arab perspective will not allow access to desired potentials and positioning in the international arena. The UAE's brand image and reputation are firmly set due to its strategically designed and implemented soft power achievements on different and comprehensive scales.

Analysing the connection between a nation's brand and soft power, using the UAE as a case study, will answer the question, how has the UAE's soft power built the solid international UAE nation's brand? The connections and associations between soft power strategy and execution of building strong and positive nation brands will be explored, using the UAE as an example, between the years 2015–2020.

Soft power means the power of attraction to the state through the ideas, principles, morals and values it embodies and through the support it provides in the fields of human rights, culture and art, which prompts others to respect and admire the model represented by that state, because of the rich influence of soft power resources.

Nations want to draw a positive image of themselves at the international level to benefit in all political, economic, social and cultural terms, and they seek to do so through a set of primary strategies, at the forefront of which is promoting the concepts on which the state is based, the ideology it adopts, and the justifications for that adoption.

The major challenge in building a nation's brand is finding a way to communicate a single message to different audiences. The UAE overcame this challenge by adopting several strategies in which the soft power sources were deployed differently to deliver and communicate the UAE nation's brand image. In this way, the UAE implemented its soft power strategy to build a positive and concrete nation brand by using several strategies to create the baseline of its projects and initiatives.

Communication is a highly effective strategy in international public relations. It allows coherence with environment elements wherein interests and needs are exchanged, but effective communication is not based on merely transmitting a personal message – growing it requires a continuous reciprocal interactive process. The interaction strategy is a mutual activity involving processes of joint influence between parties to the communication process in which each party's actions are a catalyst for the reactions of the other party.

Persuasion seeks to change perspectives on a political, commercial, or behavioural issue. This strategy addresses emotions and is based on persuading individuals and groups.

Dialogue is used in closed and in-depth intellectual discussions about anticipated problems and crises. The occurrence, how to respond to them and address them, and the processes of implementing social responsibility programs as these are adopted. This strategy depends on the dynamic stance that the negotiating parties may take and is a fundamental element of the decision-making process.

Consensus building is used to build relationships with the external environment. This strategy is usually applied only when it is appropriate, if, say, there is a conflict of interest between parties, each of which depends for its existence on the other party.

Global cultural building seeks to engage with the masses as a single, homogeneous audience, taking advantage of the various similarities between cultures. This strategy is based on the belief that culture is a comprehensive vision of the world embodied in concepts.

The external media strategy is based on the process of explaining and clarifying facts and information to audiences abroad with a goal and is one of the strategies adopted by the UAE: making an impact on the thought-processing abilities of these audiences in a way that serves the state's causes and interests. It depends on the rule that the state or its representatives can influence other countries' politics through foreign media, called open or popular diplomacy, relying on three-dimensional pillars: it is represented by the government influencing the citizens of another country, then by these individuals influencing their governments, and then by establishing a government role.

Domestic global strategy depends on organizations adapting their activities to suit the local conditions in each country.

The UAE has been dealing with soft power theory since its inception as one of the tools of its personality. As this diplomacy, or soft power, gave the UAE a position in world public opinion of the state's stances, it also strengthened the emotional image of it as a successful and highly credible country, a soft power projected by the Emirati people themselves.

The UAE enjoys a prominent position at both Arab and international levels. Its leadership aims to strengthen this position further and invest UAE cultural, humanitarian and economic efforts for the good of UAE citizens and the world's people. The UAE seeks to build strong and reliable relationships with all honourable people.

The UAE's soft power council is deploying the concept of soft power to achieve goals using the power of attraction, polarization, and acceptance of the state's culture, policy and political norms instead of coercion or financial power.

The soft power of any state is based mainly on moral mechanisms and methods, and this includes the state's culture, its manners, arts, heritage, traditions and educational systems, and the system of values prevailing in the country, such as tolerance, love, cooperation, generosity, acceptance of others, justice and good governance.

At the same time, this concept can include other models, such as a successful economic and development model adopted by the state and its role in providing development aid to the needy, or even some foreign policies that the state adopts when they are perceived as legitimate and ethical, such as defending issues of right and justice and human rights.

So, the primary source of a state's soft power is its culture and civilizational heritage; the more this factor attracts attention, whether in its popular traditions or its supreme culture, such as education, literature and poetry, the greater the power of the soft state. Soft power tools also include leadership diplomacy, humanitarian diplomacy, scientific diplomacy and the media.

Scientific power is also an indispensable component of soft power and an essential part of scientific diplomacy. The UAE entered the history books with an unprecedented space achievement for the Arab world with the successful launch of the "Hope Probe," the Emirates Project to explore Mars, from the Tanegashima Space Centre in Japan, the first space mission to explore planets led by an Arab country, the implications of which echo around the world.

The United Arab Emirates has also begun operations of the first nuclear power reactor in the Arab world at the Barakah Nuclear Energy Plant, located in the Al Dhafra region of the Emirate of Abu Dhabi on the Arabian Gulf.

Educational missions can influence students' thinking through scholarships, enabling them to become ambassadors for the countries they study. The greater the power of attraction is in those countries for the students, the greater the impact on the nation's brand. On the one hand, the UAE has several scholarship programs which send its citizens to study abroad and help build its reputation and image abroad, while on the other, the UAE hosts leading universities such as The

Sorbonne, INSEAD and the American University, enriching the education mix.

Through these methods and mechanisms, the state can draw a positive mental image of itself among other nations and their societies, encouraging them to emulate it or even adopt its values, culture, principles and aspects of life. The United Arab Emirates has become a place of pilgrimage and a destination for millions, whether with the intention of investment, tourism, acquiring knowledge, or witnessing the progress and advancement of the UAE state in all areas of life. This attractiveness is defined by the numerous visits of nations' leaders and senior officials, exemplified by the visit of His Holiness Pope Francis I when he co-signed the "Human Fraternity Document," affirming the importance of tolerance and coexistence among human beings, regardless of religion, race, colour or creed.

Indeed, without exaggerating or personal interest, the United Arab Emirates represents one of the world's most influential countries with soft power. It embodies a pioneering development model, having achieved comprehensive development in all political, economic, social and scientific fields within a remarkably short period that cannot be measured by the age of development experiences. For other countries, which preceded the UAE by decades or even centuries, have not managed to move so rapidly and successfully from being countries whose population suffers from the scarcity of resources and hardship to one that competes for the top places in the world in most global development indicators.

The UAE has also provided a vivid and unprecedented model through its successful federal experience through voluntary choice and complete conviction of the founding fathers, may God have mercy on them, of the necessity of unity to achieve the renaissance of the UAE and overcome the challenges it faces. It also presented a pioneering model for exceptional government administration in its effectiveness, the way it manages governance, its belief in strategic planning for the future on scientific grounds, and its tireless work to achieve the happiness and well-being of citizens, including the unique inauguration of a Ministry of Happiness. Most of all, the UAE has achieved all this by having wise leadership, vision, ambition and an insistence on placing the UAE in the top echelons of all global development indicators.

The cultural dimension is the most critical factor in soft power, and the UAE has provided an admirable model by taking care of the cultural dimension and transforming itself to be the centre of Arab culture, a destination for Arab and foreign intellectuals, through book fairs and artistic, cultural and heritage events that it regularly organizes. These events, and many more like them, form bridges for global cultural communication and the awards it offers to support Arts and culture, such as the International Prize for Arabic Fiction (supported by the Booker Prize Foundation) and the Sheikh Zayed Book Prize. In addition, the UAE makes great efforts to spread and consolidate universal human cultural values, as embodied by the establishment of the Louvre Abu Dhabi Museum, the significant role of the Emirates Centre for Strategic Studies and Research and many other aspects and indicators, which have turned the UAE into a platform for creative people and intellectuals from East to West, and given it an important area of influence in the Arab, Islamic, and global cultural sphere.

As well as the many models presented by the UAE from the perspective of soft power, there are many other areas in which the state is a role model for others, at the top of which is the concept of tolerance, coexistence and acceptance of the other, probably the most crucial element among the elements of soft power. The UAE unitary model is based on these values of tolerance and acceptance of others and could not have succeeded without the presence of these values that have provided an atmosphere of cooperation, love and community stability.

The culture of tolerance and moderation characterizes Emirati society and has turned the United Arab Emirates into a wonderful destination for tourists, visitors and residents from many different parts of the world. It was not envisioned that the state would, or even could, preserve the unique state of coexistence between the children of more than 200 nationalities, states and territories who reside on its land in harmony and peace in the absence of this culture of tolerance. The most important thing is the positive mental image that people of these nationalities absorb, the atmosphere of tolerance in Emirati society, the images they take with them as they return to their homelands, and images that strengthen the Emirati tolerance model's attractiveness globally.

Spreading tolerance and combating extremism, terrorism and speeches of violence and hatred, not just at local levels but regionally and internationally, is a trait that is welcomed regionally and internationally; it adds an essential ethical dimension to the United Arab Emirates' foreign policy and strengthens its soft power. Thus, the "Emirati tolerance model" is the most crucial element in strengthening the UAE's soft power.

This positive mental image of the state as a nation of tolerance works to build bridges of cooperation and communication between different cultures and religions, and in rejecting the speech of violence, hatred and extremism, the world opens its doors to Emirati citizens without fear or hesitation: the Emirati passport has become the strongest in the world and ranks number one in the world with merit, an accurate and categorical reflection of the UAE's soft power growth on the global stage.

What distinguishes the Emirati model of tolerance is that it is a comprehensive model that has its roots in the depth of Emirati history, it nourishes the original Emirati values that the generations inherited generation after generation, strengthened and entrenched more and more by wise policies, such as those that establish laws that criminalize any prejudice to the culture of tolerance or the spreading of hate and extremism. The Emirati model establishes institutional frameworks that protect the values of tolerance and entrench them as a societal culture in parallel with its unrelenting policy of confronting extremism and terrorist groups, or others that represent the greatest threat to the values of tolerance, moderation and moderation.

It is widely known that the soft power of the UAE has had an outstanding record in many humanitarian and civilizational fields since the establishment of the state, whether through the charismatic qualities of the political leadership and its respected actions in building the state and achieving human development or through the consolidation of human values.

In general, the foundations of a state and its leadership's abilities illustrate the strengths of soft power in any country, so it varies according to each country's capabilities. For example, Brazil's soft power lies mainly in football, while Germany's soft power resides in the industrial field. Thus, every country has its own distinct aspect through which it can market itself to other peoples. The UAE is emerging as the first genuinely regional power in the Arab arena through the strength of the Emirati passport as the first-ranked passport in the Arab and non-Arab world, and this is just one of the criteria for effective soft power in today's world. It also appears in many other fields and thus is an icon to dazzle the world's peoples, outshining the region's challenges.

The latest of the UAE's remarkable stories is that it is making a great effort to represent the image of Islam through a group of institutions, research centres and initiatives that demonstrate to the world the actual true image of Islam, such as the Hidaya Centre, Sawab, Al-Muwatta and the Sheikh Zayed Grand Mosque, which is playing the much larger role of being not only a place of prayer but also one of the world's wonders of Islamic architecture.

The UAE's regional policy and its recent decision to normalize relations with Israel received excellent broad support from the international community and generated a positive outlook toward innovative solutions to crises. This bold Emirati move stirred the static, stagnant waters, changing the scene to overcome painful terms in the Arab world. Hence, the Abraham Accord comes in the context of many peace initiatives and will bring about a strategic transformation.

The peace agreement with Israel must be viewed in the context of the strategic decisions of the Emirates. The UAE initiated a world-changing move by establishing normalizing relations with Israel in order to preserve the chances for a two-state solution to create security and ensure its stability.

The Pope's visit in the spring of 2019 overthrew a huge psychological barrier in the region, and this, along with pioneering decisions in employing nuclear energy and a space project to aid international exploration of Mars, are all directions taken by a nation that understands the impact that transformative strategic decision-making opportunities create.

If soft power is the power of attraction, polarization and the power of admiration for your country, the way of life that this country lives, its economic, political and other components, and even its political leaders, then this positive reputation creates political, social and economic gains. The formation of soft power is based on several pillars, including political leadership, which is especially important for shaping the state's image in the minds of the people. Every image, movement, statement and interest of the political leadership are part of this essential yet fundamental influence in building soft power.

Another axis in building soft power is humanitarian work by contributing, as a country, to humanitarian work and feeling responsibility toward global humanitarian issues. When you have a political system with individual specifications that defend higher human values, that turns into a model that inspires others to follow it, and the nation becomes a significant player in the international system.

Humanitarian work is therefore another crucial tools of soft power, and the UAE, in this regard, has dramatically benefited from the global reputation of the late Sheikh Zayed bin Sultan Al Nahyan, given the tremendous impact he had at

Arab, regional and global levels. The image of the nation's leaders is vital in supporting the power of soft countries.

In the last century, western media, in the form of Hollywood, fought against, through its artistic output, Nazism, socialism, communism and finally terrorism while promoting capitalism and individualism, playing a fundamental role as one of the essential elements of attraction. In this way, American soft power has become an essential tool in guiding American policies, shaping and supporting its political leaders, and influencing public opinion.

The United States of America has, in the eyes of the world, consolidated its image, highlighting it as a symbol and a model for values, especially the values of democracy, freedom, social justice, respect for individuality and personal freedom. Hollywood, with its magic wand, has been able to play a fundamental role in making policies and finding solutions, as Ian Scott says in his book, "American Politics in Hollywood Films. These films gradually succeeded in shaping the democratic and institutional agenda of the United States of America." In other words, as writer Peter Rollins said, "Hollywood produced films consciously to change public opinion trends regarding political and social matters, and American cinema attacked, with the influence of political trends, fascism, Nazism, communism, terrorism and the American film industry has led to a tradition. It has an essential role in spreading American popular culture, in attracting sympathy with the American way of life, and presented an attractive model for American values, especially the values of freedom, individuality and mobility."

The nation's image, its flattering glow in others' eyes, is not a secondary matter. Instead, it is an essential basis in persuading others to submit to what we wish, voluntarily, and it is imperative to succeed in inspiring others; to make them either imitate you or be convinced of your point of view and accept what you put on the agenda, given that you have a model that they respect and feel affected by.

Therefore, the countries of the region today need to search for another option that achieves their goals and may bring back the peace lost between them. Here, the importance of the significant employment of culture emerges, as these countries contain a massive balance of common cultural stock, but on occasion, they evoke the negative, conflict-exciting part of this. The stock that increases division and fragmentation, the significant conflicts of the era of sedition, for example. This destructive and rigid cultural policy needs a complete change so that the historical parts with a human dimension are in harmony with logic and the needs of the times become the basis for building the general culture of the state.

Decision-makers in the Middle East need to realize that states do not achieve their goals and build reliable, successful nation brands by hard power only. Other types of power need to be possessed: the power of culture, thought and education, the type of prevailing governance; the effectiveness of local policies; and the nature of the values they reflect.

The effects of the Emirati soft powers are cumulative and are strengthening year after year. The state is setting examples in all the humanitarian, social and scientific fields that the rest of the world is experiencing, but the full manifestation of these efforts will take some time to be realized, perhaps the next five years or so, but the state continues to take giant leaps, especially in the field of education and research. The necessary growth in scientific study is based on local and international universities' understanding of the importance of producing students who keep abreast of rapid changes in the modern era by using all available technologies.

The state has succeeded in undertaking initiatives to establish, sponsor and support educational and cultural initiatives such as the Emirati Modern School, the establishment of the Sheikh Zayed Book Award, the International Prize for Arabic Fiction, the Million Poet Competition, the Prince of Poets Competition and many others, in addition to the development of world-class tourist attractions and brands such as the Burj Khalifa, Dubai Mall, Burj Al Arab, Palm Island, Sir Bani Yas Island, Yas Island and others too numerous to mention, giving these achievements durability in the UAE's soft influences in the scientific, cultural and economic arenas. They are capped off by the global events sector, encompassing the essential elements of soft powers that the state has been cultivating and expanding over the past years and setting the perfect example by hosting Expo 2020, a meeting place for the world's civilizations and the largest event ever held on state soil.

VII. Conclusion –
Building a Strong and
Attractive UAE Nation Brand

We conclude by re-affirming that soft power plays a vital role in developing the reputation and image of states regionally and globally; state-level branding of soft power is increasingly crucial to building a nation's image as the least expensive and most appropriate and effectual option in the long term to achieve the UAE's interests and enhance its position regionally and internationally.

Today's image and attractiveness depend significantly on the strength of a nation's domestic and international values and policies: their soft power. This power not only enhances the external position of the state but also enhances its internal standing by boosting the confidence of its citizens in themselves, their political system and their future.

Therefore, countries need to develop their soft power capabilities to avoid being subject to continuous pressure, pushing them to a permanent state of instability that causes them to be reshaped in a manner inconsistent with the interests of their people, especially with the openness created by the challenges of globalization in its various forms and the spontaneous or deliberate impulse of these challenges to cultures, ideologies and policies that may sometimes threaten the national security of countries.

The Middle East is facing severe challenges and is undergoing real changes, some of which result from inter-regional actors and others are the result of interaction with the complex, intertwined and profound developments taking place in the international field. In light of this critical situation, it has even become necessary to reconsider old strategies and policies that have proven to fail. Provided that there is a willingness to adopt new strategies and policies consistent with the needs of people and the size of the challenges they face, then the combination of a reasonable formidable force and a soft, attractive force will be one of the smart and correct options to chart the path toward a better future for the governments and peoples of the region.

The robust soft power strategic planning and implementation across the UAE's entities and its citizens have played a significant role in generating the desired powerful and positive brand image.

Nevertheless, a question still remains: Who is the person or entity responsible for the national brand? Is it commercial or media entities, the private sector, or a mixture of all of these entities? Additionally, how can indicators be created that can accurately measure this, whether in terms of impact and existing international indicators or the effect of foreign policies and the extent of their success and the reflection of all this on the state's private sector?

Finding the measurement tool to assess soft power sources' impact on the success of building a national brand must remain a matter of perception. Likewise, measuring the amount of effort spent on executing a soft power strategy is imprecise by its very nature, since it is set by a combination of various government and non-government organizations.

However, one thing is clear: the UAE analysis answers positively the question of how crucially important the ownership of soft power is to build a strong and attractive UAE nation brand, which in turn answers the initial research question. The UAE nation's brand is strong and attractive, associated with its positive image in different fields locally, regionally and internationally.

Appendix: List of References

- Aldroubi, Mina. 2018. *UAE to take international lead on soft power.* December 27. https://www.thenational.ae/world/gcc/uae-to-take-international-lead-on-soft-power-1.806868. Accessed June 05, 2020.

- AlHaddad, Yousef. 2017. "UAE Soft Power Council: A Framework to Highlight the Image of the Country and Strengthen its Position." Nation Shield: 54–59. Accessed May 29, 2020.

- Almezaini K. *The UAE and foreign policy: foreign aid, identities and interests*, London: Routledge 2012.

- Anholt S. "Nation-Brands of the Twenty-First Century."

- Anholt, S. *Brand America: the mother of all brands.* Cyan Communications 2005.

- Anholt, S. *Brand New Justice. The Upside of Global Branding.* London: Butter-worth-Heinemann, 2003.

- Anholt, S. *Competitive identity: the new brand management for nations, cities and regions.* New York: Palgrave Macmillan 2007.

- Anholt, Simon "Nation As Brand." Journal of Brand Management 9 (4–5): 229–239, 2002.

- Anholt, Simon. "What is competitive identity?" In *Competitive identity*, pp. 1–23. Palgrave Macmillan, London, 2007.
- Anholt, Simon. Nation-Brands of the Twenty-First Century, Journal of Brand Management, 1998.
- Apodaca C. Foreign aid as a foreign policy tool, Oxford research encyclopedia, 2017.
- Baldwin D. *Foreign Aid, Intervention, and Influence*, World Politics, April 1, 1969, Vol 21.
- Baldwin, David A. "Modern Power Analysis." In *Power and International Relations: A Conceptual Approach*, 11–48. Princeton; Oxford: Princeton University Press, 2016.
- Bristol, Lee Hastings, ed. *Developing the corporate image: A management guide to public relations*. New York: Scribner, 1960.
- Browning, Christopher. "Nation Branding, National Self-Esteem, and the Constitution of Subjectivity in Late Modernity." Foreign Policy Analysis. 11. 10.1111/fpa.12028. 2013.
- Cantor, Robert D. *Contemporary international politics*. West Group, 1986.
- Chandrasekaran R. In the UAE, the United States has a quiet, potent ally nicknamed 'Little Sparta,' Washington Post, 2014. https://www.washingtonpost.com/world/national-security/in-the-uae-the-united-states-has-a-quiet-potent-ally-nicknamed-little-sparta/2014/11/08/3fc6a50c-643a-11e4-836c-

83bc4f26eb67_story.html?noredirect=on&utm_term=.5014403859a9

- Cox Michael, Stokes Doug. *US Foreign Policy*. Glasgow: Oxford University Press, 2018.
- Dinnie, Keith. *Nation branding: Concepts, issues, practice*. Routledge, 2015.
- Fan, Y. Branding the nation: Toward a better understanding. Place Branding and Public Diplomacy, 2010.
- Fan, Ying. "Branding the nation: What is being branded." Journal of Vacation Marketing, Volume 12, No. 1, 2005.
- Fukuyama, Francis. *The End of history and Last Man*. London: Penguin Books, 2012.
- Gallarotti, Giulio M. "Soft power: what it is, why it's important, and the conditions for its effective use." *Journal of Political Power* 4, no. 1 (2011): 25–47.
- Gienow-Hecht, J.C.E. *Nation Branding*. Cambridge University Press, 2016.
- Gudjonsson, Hlynur. "Nation branding." *Place branding* 1, no. 3 (2005): 283–298.
- Henry, Frederick. Hard and Soft Power: The Paradox of "Winning the War of Ideas" in the 21st Century, 29, 2005.
- Hvidt M. The Dubai model: an outline of key development process elements in Dubai, International journal of Middle East studies, Vol 4. 2009.

- Jaffe, Eugene D., and Israel D. Nebenzahl. *National Image ND Competitive Advantage: The Theory and Practice of Country-of-origin Effect.* Copenhagen business school press, 2001.

- Journal of Brand Management, 1998.

- Kaneva, N. Nation branding: Toward an agenda of critical research. International Journal of Communication, 2011.

- Kanna, M. 2014. "Emirati foreign aid: Overview and foreign policy implications." honours thesis paper 35. https://scholarworks.wm.edu/honorthesis/35.

- Kearn Jr, David W. "The power curse: influence & illusion in world politics." (2010): 275–282.

- Keohane, R.O. and Nye, J.S. 1989, *Power and interdependence: World politics in transition. 3rd ed.* Boston: Little-Brown.

- Kerr, Pauline, and Wiseman, Geoffrey. *Diplomacy in a Globalizing World: Theories and Practices.* 2013.

- Khan, Asad Ullah. "Pakistan's Strategy of Countering Violent Extremism: Need for Soft Power." *Strategic Studies* 37, no. 3 (2017): 156–67. Accessed June 5, 2020. doi:10.2307/48537563.

- Kotler, Philip, and Kevin Lane Keller. "Marketing Management. New Jersey: Preason Prentice Hall." (2012).

- Lukes, Steven. "Power and the battle for hearts and minds: on the bluntness of soft power." In *Power in world politics*, pp. 83–97. Routledge Taylor & Francis Group, 2007.

- Marks, Michael. *Metaphors in international relations theory*. Springer, 2011.
- Mattern, Janice Bially. "Why soft power isn't so soft: representational force and the sociolinguistic construction of attraction in world politics." *Millennium* 33, no. 3 (2005): 583–612.
- McDermott, Rose. *Political psychology in international relations*. University of Michigan Press, 2004.
- Mearsheimer, John J. *China's Unpeaceful Rise.* Current history, Research library, 2006.
- Mearsheimer, John J. *The Tragedy of Great Power Politics.* New York: W.W. Norton & Company, 2003.
- Melissen, Jan. *The new public diplomacy: soft power in international relations.* New York: Palgrave Macmillan, 2005.
- Melissen. Jan. 2009. *The New Public Diplomacy: Between Theory and Practice.* Oxford Press Revised Edition.
- Monten, Jonathan. "Thucydides and Modern Realism." *International Studies Quarterly* 50, no. 1 (2006): 3–25. Accessed June 10, 2020. www.jstor.org/stable/3693549.
- Morgenthau, H. J. *Politics Among Nations.* New York: Chicago Press, 1962.
- Morgenthau, Hans Joachim, Kenneth W. Thompson, and W. David Clinton. "Politics among nations: The struggle for power and peace." 1985.

- Niall, Ferguson. "Think Again: Power." *Foreign Policy* (2013).
- Nobel, Jaap W. "Morgenthau's Struggle with Power: The Theory of Power Politics and the Cold War." *Review of International Studies* 21, no. 1 (1995): 61–85. Accessed June 9, 2020. www.jstor.org/stable/20097396.
- Nye J. "Notes for a Soft-Power Research Agenda." In *Power in World Politics*, edited by Felix Berenskoetter and M. J. Williams. New York: Routledge, 2007.
- Nye J. *Soft Power: The Means to Success in World Politics*, New York: Public Affairs, 2004.
- Nye J. *Soft Power: The means to Success in World Politics*. New York: Public Affairs, 2004.
- Nye, Jr, Joseph S. *Soft power: The means to success in world politics*. Public affairs, 2004.
- Nye, J. *Bound to Lead: the Changing Nature of American Power*. New York: 1990.
- Nye, J. S.,2005. Dunya siyasetinde basarinin yolu: Yumusak guc [Soft power: The means to success in world politics].1st edition. Istanbul: Elips Kitap.
- Nye, Joseph S. "Get Smart: Combining Hard and Soft Power." Foreign Affairs 88, no. 4 (2009): 160–63. Accessed June 5, 2020. www.jstor.org/stable/20699631.
- Nye, Joseph S. *Soft Power: The Means to Success in World Politics*. 1st ed. 2004.

- Nye, Joseph S. *Soft Power: the means to success in world politics.* New York: Public Affairs, 2004 1st edition.
- Nye, Joseph, and Alan Philps. "Joseph Nye." *The World Today*69, no. 3 (2013): 32–34. Accessed June 5, 2020. www.jstor.org/stable/41963167.
- Olins, Wally. "Branding the Nation – The Historical Context." Journal of Brand Management 9 (4–5): 241–248. 2002.
- Olins, Wally. *Corporate identity: Making business strategy visible through design.* Harvard Business School Pr, 1990.
- Rendon, Jim. "When Nations Need a Little Marketing," New York Times. 2003.
- Reus-Smit, Christian and Sanidal Duncan, "The Oxford Handbook of International Relations," 2010.
- Ricketts, Rita, and Joseph S. Nye. "Winning The Match Point" *New Zealand International Review* 33, no. 6 (2008): 7–11. Accessed June 5, 2020. doi:10.2307/45235843.
- Riston, M. "Liechtenstein's Five Steps to Superficial Change," Marketing Journal, 2004.
- Rothman, Steven B. "Revising the soft power concept: what are the means and mechanisms of soft power?" *Journal of Political Power* 4, no. 1 (2011): 49–64.
- Shah, A. 2014. Foreign aid for development assistance. http://www.globalissues.org/article/35/foreign-aid-development-assistance. Accessed May 29, 2020.

- Soubrier, Emma. "Evolving Foreign and Security Policies: A Comparative Study of Qatar and the UAE," in: Khalid Almezaini et Jean-Marc Rickli (dir.), "The Gulf Small States: Foreign and Security Policies, Londres: Routledge, 2016." (2016).
- Surowiec, Pawel. *Nation branding, public relations and soft power: Corporatising Poland.* Routledge, 2016.
- Syros, Vasileios. "'Soft' And 'Hard' Power In Islamic Political Advice Literature." In *Violence in Islamic Thought from the Mongols to European Imperialism*, edited by Gleave Robert and Kristó-Nagy István T., 165–90. Edinburgh: Edinburgh University Press, 2018. Accessed June 5, 2020. www.jstor.org/stable/10.3366/j.ctt1tqxvdf.14.
- UAE Embassy, social and cultural ties. https://www.uae-embassy.org/uae-us-relations/key-areas-bilateral-cooperation/social-and-cultural.
- UAE Government, Portal. 2019. "The UAE Soft Power Strategy." *The United Arab Emirates' Government portal.* https://government.ae/en/about-the-uae/strategies-initiatives-and-awards/federal-governments-strategies-and-plans/the-uae-soft-power-strategy.
- Van Ham, Peter. "Place branding: The state of the art." *The Annals of the American Academy of Political and Social Science* 616, no. 1 (2008): 126–149.
- Van, Ham. "Branding European Power." Place Branding and Public Diplomacy 1. 122–126. 2005.

- Vaughan, Geoffrey M. "The Audience Of "Leviathan" and the Audience Of Hobbes's Political Philosophy." *History of Political Thought* 22, no. 3 (2001): 448–71. Accessed June 10, 2020. www.jstor.org/stable/26219797.
- Vibert, Frank. "Soft Power and international rule-making (2008)."
- Vuving, Alexander. "How soft power works." *Available at SSRN 1466220* (2009).
- Walker, Christopher. "The Hijacking of 'Soft Power.'" Journal of Democracy, 2016.
- Waltz, Kenneth N. *Realism and International Politics*. New York: Routledge, Taylor & Francis Group, 2008.
- Wang, Jian. *Soft Power, Nation Branding, and the World Expo.* In Shaping China's Global imagination. Palgrave Macmillan Series in Global Public Diplomacy. New York: Palgrave Macmillan, 2013. Pages 1–21.
- Wang, Yiwei. "Public Diplomacy and the Rise of Chinese Soft Power." *The Annals of the American Academy of Political and Social Science,* 2008.
- Young, Karen E. "A new politics of GCC economic statecraft: The case of UAE aid and financial intervention in Egypt." *Journal of Arabian Studies* 7, no. 1 (2017): 113–136.